AF492407

THIS BOOK IS DEDICATED TO THE
Stephen G. family,
(Author) Stephen G.

Table of Contents

Mars Awaits: Elon Musk's Vision for Human Life Beyond Earth

Chapter 1: The Early Years of Elon Musk Childhood and Family Background

Elon Musk was born on June 28, 1971, in Pretoria, South Africa, to a family that would play a significant role in shaping his future pursuits in technology and entrepreneurship. His father, Errol Musk, was an electromechanical engineer, pilot, and sailor, while his mother, Maye Musk, was a model and dietitian. Growing up in a household that valued intellect and creativity, Musk was encouraged to explore his interests from an early age. His family dynamic, characterized by his parents' diverse talents and ambitions, laid a foundation for his relentless drive and innovative thinking.

Musk's early life in South Africa was marked by a mix of privilege and challenges. He exhibited an early passion for technology, frequently immersing himself in books and developing an interest in computing. By the age of 12, he had already created and sold a video game called Blastar, showcasing his entrepreneurial spirit. However, Musk's childhood was not without its difficulties; he faced bullying at school and struggled with social interactions, experiences that would later inform his understanding of resilience and determination in the face of adversity.

In 1989, at the age of 17, Musk made a pivotal decision to leave South Africa and pursue opportunities in the United States and Canada. He moved to Canada to live with his mother, who had relocated there for work. This transition marked a significant turning point in Musk's life, as he sought to escape the limitations he felt in his home country. He enrolled at Queen's University in Kingston, Ontario, and later transferred to the University of Pennsylvania, where he earned degrees in both physics and economics. This academic foundation was instrumental in preparing him for the entrepreneurial ventures that lay ahead.

Musk's family background and early experiences provided him with a unique perspective on innovation and technology. His father's engineering expertise and his mother's emphasis on health and well-being influenced Musk's approach to problem-solving and sustainable living. The combination of these influences, together with his education, helped him develop a vision that transcended conventional boundaries, positioning him to tackle some of the most pressing challenges facing humanity.

As Musk embarked on his career, the values instilled in him during his formative years became evident in his ventures. From co-founding Zip2 and PayPal to establishing SpaceX and Tesla, Musk's relentless pursuit of innovation can be traced back to his upbringing. His childhood experiences with adversity and his family's emphasis on exploration and learning formed the bedrock of his ambition to not only advance technology but also envision a future where humanity thrives beyond Earth.

Education and Interests

Elon Musk's education and interests have played a pivotal role in shaping his innovative mindset and entrepreneurial ventures. Born in Pretoria, South Africa, Musk displayed an affinity for technology and entrepreneurship from a young age. His early life was marked by an insatiable curiosity and a strong inclination towards reading. By the age of 12, he had already taught himself computer programming, creating a video game called Blastar that he sold for approximately $500. This early experience not only foreshadowed his later successes but also established a lifelong pattern of self-directed learning and exploration in technology.

Musk's formal education began at Queen's University in Canada and later continued at the University of Pennsylvania, where he earned degrees in both physics and economics. His time at Penn was crucial in fostering his interest in the intersection of technology and business. The rigorous academic environment allowed him to delve into complex scientific theories while also understanding the dynamics of economic systems. This dual focus would later inform his approach to founding and growing companies like Zip2 and PayPal, where he applied both technical expertise and business acumen to drive innovation.

The founding of Zip2 marked Musk's first significant foray into entrepreneurship. The company provided online city guide software to newspapers, and Musk's vision was instrumental in its growth. His technical knowledge, combined with a keen understanding of market needs, enabled him to navigate the early internet landscape effectively. The success of Zip2 culminated in its acquisition by Compaq for nearly $300 million, providing Musk with the capital needed to pursue his subsequent ventures. This experience not only solidified his reputation in the tech industry but also instilled a belief in the transformative power of technology to solve real-world problems.

Musk's role in the rise of PayPal further exemplifies how his education and interests converged to influence his career trajectory. As co-founder of X.com, which later became PayPal, he was at the forefront of revolutionizing online payments. His vision for a seamless, secure online transaction system reflected his understanding of both consumer behavior and technological capabilities. The success of PayPal not only provided Musk with significant financial resources but also established him as a key player in the tech industry, paving the way for his ambitious projects in space exploration and sustainable energy.

Throughout his career, Musk's interests have consistently aligned with his educational background, driving his endeavors in companies like SpaceX, Tesla, Neuralink, and The Boring Company. His commitment to addressing global challenges, such as climate change and the need for interplanetary colonization, is rooted in the scientific principles he studied and the entrepreneurial spirit he developed. By integrating his education with his passions, Musk has not only influenced modern technology and entrepreneurship but has also inspired a new generation to dream beyond the confines of Earth, embodying the essence of innovation that defines his legacy.

Early Influences and Inspirations

Elon Musk's early influences and inspirations played a significant role in shaping his ambitious vision for the future. Born in Pretoria, South Africa, in 1971, Musk was exposed to technology and entrepreneurship from a young age. His father, Errol Musk, was an electromechanical engineer, while his mother, Maye Musk, was a dietitian and model. This environment fostered an early interest in science and technology, as Musk often found himself tinkering with electronics and computers. His voracious reading habits also set him apart; he consumed books on a wide array of topics, including science fiction, which would later influence his aspirations for space travel and interplanetary colonization.

Musk's move to Canada at the age of 17 marked a pivotal transition in his life. He attended Queen's University and later transferred to the University of Pennsylvania, where he earned degrees in both physics and economics. His educational background laid a strong foundation for his future endeavors in technology and business. During his college years, Musk was inspired by the works of visionaries like Nikola Tesla and Thomas Edison, whose innovations in electricity and energy systems resonated with Musk's own ambitions. This fascination with groundbreaking technologies would later manifest in his pursuits with Tesla, SpaceX, and other ventures aimed at transforming industries.

The founding of Zip2 in 1996 was a critical step in Musk's entrepreneurial journey. The company, which provided online business directories and maps, capitalized on the growing internet boom and showcased Musk's ability to identify and seize opportunities in emerging markets. The success of Zip2 also highlighted Musk's knack for navigating the tech landscape, ultimately leading to its acquisition by Compaq for approximately $307 million in 1999. This windfall not only provided Musk with the capital to invest in future projects but also solidified his reputation as a forward-thinking entrepreneur.

Following the sale of Zip2, Musk co-founded X.com, which would later become PayPal. This venture was instrumental in revolutionizing online payments and showcased Musk's commitment to leveraging technology for practical solutions. Under his leadership, PayPal became a leader in digital payments, emphasizing security and user experience. The experience gained from X.com and its subsequent sale to eBay for $1.5 billion further propelled Musk's career, allowing him to explore more ambitious projects in space and energy, aligning closely with his long-held vision of making life multi-planetary.

Throughout his career, Musk's early influences and inspirations have remained central to his identity as an innovator and entrepreneur. His childhood experiences, education, and initial ventures laid the groundwork for his later successes with SpaceX, Tesla, and beyond. The integration of technological advancement with a visionary approach to solving global challenges reflects Musk's lifelong pursuit of creating a sustainable future for humanity. As he continues to push the boundaries of what is possible, the foundational influences from his early years serve as a testament to the power of inspiration in shaping one's destiny.

Chapter 2: The Genesis of Zip2
Founding Zip2

Elon Musk's journey into entrepreneurship began with the founding of Zip2 in 1996, a company that would lay the groundwork for his future ventures. Zip2 was conceived as a city guide software for newspapers, providing businesses with an online presence and helping consumers find local services. Musk, along with his brother Kimbal and their partner Greg Kouri, saw the potential of the internet to transform how information was disseminated. They aimed to capitalize on the burgeoning digital landscape by offering a platform that would bridge the gap between traditional print media and the emerging online world.

The early days of Zip2 were marked by significant challenges. Musk and his team worked tirelessly, often putting in long hours to develop the software and secure partnerships with newspapers. The company's initial struggles included convincing traditional media outlets of the value of an online presence. However, Musk's relentless drive and vision helped him navigate these hurdles. He focused on building a robust product that would not only meet the needs of consumers but also appeal to businesses eager to leverage the internet for marketing and customer engagement.

As Zip2 grew, so did its influence in the tech industry. The company attracted attention and investment, which allowed for rapid expansion. Musk's leadership style was characterized by high expectations and a commitment to innovation, which fostered a culture of creativity within the team. They developed features that went beyond simple listings, incorporating maps and directions, thus enhancing the user experience. This forward-thinking approach positioned Zip2 as a pioneer in the online business directory space, setting the stage for future advancements in digital marketing.

In 1999, Zip2's success culminated in a significant acquisition by Compaq for approximately $307 million. This sale not only provided Musk with considerable financial resources but also solidified his reputation as a successful entrepreneur. The experience gained from building and selling Zip2 proved invaluable for Musk, as it equipped him with insights into technology, business strategy, and the intricacies of navigating the startup landscape. This early chapter in Musk's career served as a stepping stone, propelling him toward subsequent ventures like X.com, which would later evolve into PayPal.

The founding of Zip2 marked the beginning of Elon Musk's transformation from a young entrepreneur with a vision into a formidable force in the tech world. The lessons learned during this period, particularly in terms of innovation, perseverance, and strategic thinking, became cornerstones of Musk's future endeavors. As he ventured into aerospace with SpaceX and electric vehicles with Tesla, the foundational skills and experiences gleaned from Zip2 continued to influence his approach to innovation and ambition, ultimately shaping his vision for a future beyond Earth.

Challenges and Breakthroughs

Elon Musk's journey has been characterized by a series of challenges that have tested his resolve and ingenuity. From his early ventures with Zip2, where he faced significant skepticism from investors and competitors, to the tumultuous beginnings of PayPal, Musk encountered numerous obstacles. His relentless pursuit of innovation often put him at odds with established norms in the tech industry, leading to intense public scrutiny and pressure. Each setback, however, became a pivotal learning experience, shaping his approach to future endeavors and reinforcing his belief in the importance of resilience in the face of adversity.

The formation of SpaceX epitomizes the breakthroughs that Musk achieved after overcoming numerous challenges. Faced with the daunting task of developing a reusable rocket system, Musk and his team initially struggled with multiple launch failures. These setbacks could have discouraged many, but Musk's tenacity led to critical innovations that ultimately revolutionized space travel. The successful launch of Falcon 9 in 2010 marked a turning point not only for SpaceX but also for the aerospace industry, showcasing Musk's vision of reducing the cost of access to space and paving the way for future interplanetary exploration.

Tesla, another of Musk's flagship projects, faced its own set of challenges, particularly in its early years. The transition from the initial Roadster to the more ambitious Model S was fraught with production delays, financial hurdles, and market skepticism. However, Musk's commitment to sustainable energy and electric vehicles propelled Tesla to become a leader in the automotive industry. His innovative approach to manufacturing and design, coupled with strategic partnerships and a strong focus on customer satisfaction, enabled Tesla to break through barriers that many thought insurmountable.

In more recent years, Musk has ventured into the realms of Neuralink and The Boring Company, where he has encountered unique challenges related to technological advancement and regulatory approval. Neuralink's pursuit of brain-computer interfaces has raised ethical questions and requires navigating complex medical and scientific landscapes. Meanwhile, The Boring Company aims to redefine urban transportation through tunneling technology, facing skepticism from both the public and city officials about its feasibility. Despite these hurdles, Musk's ability to envision the potential of these projects continues to inspire innovation and exploration in fields that many consider speculative.

Musk's vision for Mars colonization encapsulates the ultimate breakthrough that he aspires to achieve. While the challenges of establishing a human presence on another planet are monumental—ranging from life support systems to sustainable habitats—Musk remains undeterred. His plans for SpaceX's Starship and the broader colonization efforts spotlight his determination to make interplanetary life a reality. As he navigates these challenges, Musk's journey serves as a testament to the power of vision and perseverance, inspiring future generations to pursue their own bold ambitions in the face of uncertainty.

Acquisition and Impact on Musk's Career

Elon Musk's career trajectory was significantly influenced by the acquisition of his company, PayPal, by eBay in 2002. This event marked a pivotal moment in Musk's professional life, providing him with both capital and newfound recognition in the tech industry. The sale was valued at approximately $1.5 billion, and Musk, who was the largest shareholder at the time, received a substantial payout that would later fuel his ambitious ventures. This financial windfall not only alleviated the pressures of startup life but also positioned him as a key player in Silicon Valley, where he could leverage his wealth to explore groundbreaking ideas.

The impact of the PayPal acquisition on Musk's career extended beyond monetary gain. It allowed him to shift his focus from online payment systems to more ambitious projects that aligned with his long-term vision for humanity. With the resources acquired from the sale, Musk founded SpaceX in 2002, driven by his desire to make space travel more affordable and ultimately enable the colonization of Mars. This transition exemplified Musk's ability to pivot quickly and seize opportunities that aligned with his overarching goal of advancing human life beyond Earth.

Moreover, the acquisition solidified Musk's reputation as an entrepreneur capable of successfully launching and scaling tech companies. The experience garnered from PayPal, where he navigated challenges related to growth and competition, equipped him with invaluable insights into running a successful business. This knowledge proved essential as he faced the numerous obstacles at SpaceX and later at Tesla. The critical thinking and problem-solving skills honed during his tenure at PayPal became instrumental when tackling issues such as rocket development failures and production bottlenecks in the automotive sector.

In addition to his entrepreneurial skills, the PayPal acquisition allowed Musk to cultivate a network of influential connections within the tech community. Many of his former colleagues went on to play significant roles in his later ventures, fostering a collaborative environment that drove innovation. This interconnectedness not only facilitated knowledge exchange but also provided Musk with a support system that was crucial during the early, often tumultuous phases of SpaceX and Tesla. The relationships built during his PayPal days laid the groundwork for a robust ecosystem that would support his future endeavors.

Ultimately, the acquisition of PayPal was more than just a financial milestone for Elon Musk; it was a transformative event that reshaped his career and ambitions. It enabled him to shift his focus toward revolutionary projects that would define the landscape of technology and space exploration in the 21st century. Musk emerged not only as a successful entrepreneur but also as a visionary leader whose aspirations extended far beyond profit, aiming instead for the advancement of human civilization and the exploration of new frontiers. This pivotal moment set the stage for the ambitious pursuits that would follow, marking the inception of Musk's journey toward making life multi-planetary.

Chapter 3: The PayPal Revolution
Joining X.com

Joining X.com marked a pivotal moment in Elon Musk's career, setting the stage for his future endeavors in technology and entrepreneurship. Founded in 1999, X.com was initially conceived as an online banking platform aimed at revolutionizing the financial services industry. Musk's vision was to create a one-stop shop for banking needs, offering everything from checking accounts to investment services, all through the convenience of the internet. This ambition aligned with the burgeoning tech landscape of the late 1990s, where the dot-com boom was transforming how people interacted with financial institutions.

The early days of X.com were fraught with challenges, as Musk faced the complexities of navigating a highly regulated industry. Despite these obstacles, he managed to assemble a talented team of engineers and financial experts who shared his vision. The innovative approach Musk championed emphasized user experience and security, which were critical for gaining the trust of potential customers. His leadership style, characterized by a willingness to take risks and embrace new ideas, helped to foster a culture of creativity and problem-solving within the fledgling company.

In March 2000, X.com merged with Confinity, a company that had developed a money-transfer service known as PayPal. This merger proved to be a turning point, as the combined resources and expertise allowed the company to pivot towards a more focused mission: simplifying online payments. The PayPal platform quickly gained traction, and under Musk's leadership, the company refined its services to create a seamless transaction experience. This shift not only solidified PayPal's position in the market but also laid the groundwork for Musk's future successes in the tech industry.

As PayPal grew, it attracted significant attention from investors and tech enthusiasts alike. The platform became synonymous with online payments, effectively changing the way people conducted financial transactions on the internet. The success of PayPal, culminating in its acquisition by eBay in 2002, provided Musk with both financial resources and increased visibility in the tech world. This experience was instrumental in shaping his understanding of scaling a business and the importance of innovation in maintaining relevance in rapidly evolving industries.

Musk's journey with X.com and PayPal not only established him as a formidable player in the tech landscape but also equipped him with valuable lessons that he would carry into his later ventures, including SpaceX and Tesla. The emphasis on innovation, risk-taking, and user-centric design became hallmarks of his approach to entrepreneurship. Joining X.com was more than just a career move for Musk; it was a significant step toward realizing his broader vision of transforming industries and ultimately, humanity's future beyond Earth.

The Merger with Confinity

The merger between X.com, founded by Elon Musk, and Confinity, which developed the money transfer service known as PayPal, marked a pivotal moment in the evolution of online financial transactions. Initially launched in 1999, X.com aimed to revolutionize banking by providing an online platform for various financial services. Confinity, on the other hand, had a more focused approach, concentrating on creating a digital wallet for Palm Pilots and facilitating person-to-person payments. The convergence of these two companies was driven by a shared vision of simplifying and democratizing financial transactions in the digital age.

The merger took place in March 2000, during a time when both companies faced significant challenges in a burgeoning tech landscape. X.com was struggling to gain traction and was in need of a robust product to build upon, while Confinity was experiencing its own difficulties in capturing a larger market share. By joining forces, the newly formed entity, which retained the PayPal name, combined X.com's ambitious vision and financial backing with Confinity's established technology and user base. This strategic alliance allowed the combined company to streamline its operations and enhance its product offerings, ultimately positioning it as a leader in the online payment industry.

Elon Musk's role in the merger was significant, as he was an advocate for innovation and aggressive growth strategies. However, the consolidation was not without its internal conflicts. Musk's vision often clashed with the leadership styles and priorities of the Confinity co-founders, particularly Peter Thiel and Max Levchin. Tensions escalated, leading to Musk's ousting as CEO just months after the merger. Despite this setback, Musk remained involved as a key stakeholder and continued to influence the company's strategic direction, which helped to accelerate its growth trajectory.

Under the PayPal brand, the company experienced rapid expansion and success, ultimately becoming a household name in online payments. The platform's ease of use and innovative features attracted millions of users, transforming the way people conducted financial transactions. The merger not only solidified Musk's reputation as a visionary entrepreneur but also laid the groundwork for the future of digital finance. PayPal's success paved the way for significant advancements in e-commerce, enabling countless businesses and individuals to engage in secure online transactions.

The legacy of the merger with Confinity extends beyond just financial technology. It exemplifies Musk's ability to adapt and persevere in the face of adversity, a trait that would define his career. The experience gained during this pivotal time informed Musk's later ventures, including SpaceX and Tesla, where he would again challenge traditional industries and push the boundaries of innovation. The merger thus stands as a crucial chapter in Musk's journey, highlighting the intersection of technology, entrepreneurship, and the relentless pursuit of a visionary future.

PayPal's Impact on E-commerce and Musk's Future

PayPal's emergence in the late 1990s revolutionized the realm of online transactions, paving the way for the burgeoning e-commerce landscape. As a co-founder of X.com, which later became PayPal, Elon Musk was instrumental in this transformation. His vision of a secure and efficient online payment system aligned with the growing demand for digital transactions, which were becoming essential as more consumers began to engage with e-commerce platforms. This shift not only facilitated a new era of online shopping but also laid the groundwork for PayPal to become an integral part of the internet's infrastructure.

The impact of PayPal extended beyond mere convenience; it fundamentally changed how businesses and consumers interacted in the digital marketplace. By providing a reliable payment system, PayPal enabled small and medium-sized enterprises to enter the online space with confidence. This democratization of commerce allowed entrepreneurs to reach global audiences without the need for traditional banking systems. Musk's role in this transition was significant, as he championed innovations such as instant money transfers, which further enhanced user experience and trust.

Musk's involvement with PayPal also had profound implications for his career trajectory. After PayPal's acquisition by eBay in 2002, Musk received a substantial financial windfall, which he subsequently reinvested into his next ventures, including SpaceX and Tesla. The success of PayPal not only provided Musk with the capital he needed but also established his reputation as a visionary entrepreneur capable of transforming industries. This trajectory illustrates how PayPal served as a springboard, enabling Musk to pursue ambitious projects that would define the future of technology and space exploration.

As e-commerce continues to evolve, the principles established by PayPal remain relevant. The company's focus on security, user experience, and innovation has influenced countless startups and established businesses alike. The rise of digital wallets and cryptocurrencies can be traced back to the groundwork laid by PayPal, showcasing Musk's lasting legacy in shaping digital financial ecosystems. As e-commerce adapts to new technologies and consumer behaviors, the foundational changes initiated by PayPal will continue to resonate.

Looking ahead, Musk's vision extends beyond Earth, encompassing the colonization of Mars and the establishment of a multi-planetary society. The lessons learned from PayPal's impact on e-commerce will undoubtedly inform how future transactions and economies are structured in space. As humanity ventures into new frontiers, the principles of secure, efficient payments that Musk helped to pioneer will play a crucial role in supporting commerce and community building on other planets. Thus, PayPal's impact on e-commerce not only reflects Musk's past achievements but also serves as a critical component of his futuristic aspirations.

Chapter 4: SpaceX: A New Frontier
Founding SpaceX

In 2002, Elon Musk founded Space Exploration Technologies Corp., commonly known as SpaceX, with the ambitious goal of reducing space transportation costs and enabling the colonization of Mars. This venture was born out of Musk's longstanding fascination with space and his belief that humanity must become a multiplanetary species. He envisioned a future where humans could live on other planets, primarily Mars, and saw SpaceX as the vehicle to realize this dream. The early days of the company were marked by significant challenges, including funding difficulties and skepticism from the aerospace industry, which had long been dominated by established giants like NASA and Lockheed Martin.

Musk invested $100 million of his own fortune into SpaceX in its formative years, demonstrating his commitment to the mission despite the risks involved. The company's initial focus was on the development of the Falcon 1 rocket, a small and cost-effective launch vehicle. In 2006, the first Falcon 1 launch ended in failure, followed by two more unsuccessful attempts in 2007 and 2008. Each setback tested Musk's resolve, but his determination to succeed remained unwavering. These early failures ultimately laid the groundwork for future successes, as the team learned valuable lessons that would guide the development of subsequent rockets.

The breakthrough came in July 2009 when Falcon 1 successfully reached orbit, making SpaceX the first privately funded company to do so. This achievement not only validated Musk's vision but also opened the door for commercial contracts with NASA and other entities. In 2012, SpaceX made history again by becoming the first private company to deliver cargo to the International Space Station (ISS) with its Dragon spacecraft. This milestone was pivotal in demonstrating the viability of commercial spaceflight and solidified SpaceX's reputation as a leader in the aerospace sector.

SpaceX continued to innovate, developing the Falcon 9 rocket and the Dragon 2 spacecraft, which would eventually carry astronauts to the ISS as part of NASA's Commercial Crew Program. The introduction of reusable rocket technology marked a significant turning point in space exploration, drastically lowering the cost of access to space. The successful landing of the Falcon 9 first stage after launch signified a new era in rocketry, allowing for rapid reusability and enhancing the economic feasibility of space missions. This innovation not only transformed SpaceX but also challenged conventional norms in the aerospace industry.

Through relentless innovation and a bold vision, SpaceX has transformed the landscape of space exploration. The company's achievements have inspired a new generation of entrepreneurs and engineers, encouraging them to think beyond traditional boundaries. Musk's ambition to colonize Mars continues to drive SpaceX's projects, including the development of the Starship spacecraft, designed for deep space missions and human settlement on Mars. As SpaceX forges ahead, the legacy of its founding sets the stage for a future where humanity expands its reach beyond Earth, fulfilling Musk's vision of a multiplanetary civilization.

Early Challenges and Setbacks

Elon Musk's journey to becoming a prominent figure in technology and space exploration was not without its early challenges and setbacks. After moving to the United States from South Africa, Musk faced the daunting task of establishing himself in a competitive environment. His initial foray into the tech world began with Zip2, a company he co-founded in 1996. While Zip2 offered promising potential as a city guide software for newspapers, Musk encountered significant obstacles. The company struggled to gain traction in a market that was not yet ready for its innovative approach, leading to financial pressure and a tumultuous relationship with investors and partners.

The next major chapter in Musk's career unfolded with the creation of X.com in 1999, which would later evolve into PayPal. Despite the initial excitement surrounding the concept of online banking, Musk once again faced considerable challenges. Internal disputes and conflicts with co-founders led to his temporary ousting as CEO. This setback was not only a personal blow but also a pivotal moment that forced Musk to reassess his leadership style and approach to collaboration. Though Musk would eventually return to lead the company to success, the experience underscored the volatility and unpredictability of the tech industry.

Following the sale of PayPal to eBay in 2002, Musk shifted his focus to aerospace by founding SpaceX. This venture was driven by his long-standing ambition to make space travel affordable and accessible. However, the early years of SpaceX were fraught with difficulties. The company faced numerous technical failures, including multiple rocket launch failures that threatened its survival. With limited funding and a small team, Musk had to navigate the complex world of aerospace engineering, often relying on his own ingenuity and determination to overcome the hurdles that stood in his way.

Simultaneously, Musk was also pursuing his vision for electric vehicles through Tesla Motors, which he joined in 2004. The automotive industry proved to be a different kind of battlefield, marked by skepticism regarding electric cars' viability and the immense capital required to develop new technologies. Tesla faced production delays, financial struggles, and a challenging market environment. Musk's relentless pursuit of innovation often put him at odds with investors and stakeholders, who were wary of the risks associated with his ambitious plans. Yet, these early challenges ultimately laid the groundwork for Tesla's eventual success in the electric vehicle market.

Musk's experiences during these formative years were crucial in shaping his approach to business and innovation. Each setback forced him to adapt, learn, and refine his vision for the future. His resilience and willingness to embrace risk would later become defining traits as he pursued even more audacious goals, such as colonizing Mars and developing neural interfaces. Understanding the struggles he faced in his early career provides valuable insight into the mindset of a man who has continually pushed the boundaries of what is possible, turning obstacles into stepping stones toward his grand visions for humanity's future.

Key Innovations and Milestones

The journey of Elon Musk is marked by several key innovations and milestones that have not only shaped his career but also altered the landscape of technology and space exploration. From his early ventures in the tech industry to his groundbreaking work in aerospace and electric vehicles, Musk's contributions have consistently pushed the boundaries of what is possible. One of the earliest milestones in his career was the founding of Zip2 in 1996, which provided online business directories and maps for newspapers. This venture laid the groundwork for his understanding of digital platforms and set the stage for his later successes.

Following the sale of Zip2, Musk co-founded X.com in 1999, which later became PayPal. This platform revolutionized online payments and significantly impacted e-commerce. The success of PayPal not only solidified Musk's position in the tech industry but also provided him with the financial resources to pursue his ambitious goals in space exploration and sustainable energy. The acquisition of PayPal by eBay in 2002 for $1.5 billion gave Musk the capital needed to establish SpaceX, a company that would fundamentally change the dynamics of space travel.

SpaceX, founded in 2002, marked a significant milestone in Musk's career and the history of aerospace. The company's early innovations included the development of the Falcon 1 rocket, which, in 2008, became the first privately developed liquid-fueled rocket to reach orbit. This achievement not only demonstrated the viability of privatized space exploration but also set a precedent for future missions. By 2012, SpaceX's Dragon spacecraft became the first commercial vehicle to deliver cargo to the International Space Station, showcasing the potential for private companies to partner with governmental space agencies.

In parallel with his work in aerospace, Musk's vision for sustainable energy led to the development of Tesla, Inc. The launch of the Tesla Roadster in 2008 was a pivotal moment, as it proved that electric vehicles could be both high-performance and desirable. Over the years, Tesla has evolved to include a range of electric vehicles and energy products, significantly influencing the automotive industry and driving innovation in renewable energy solutions. This evolution reflects Musk's commitment to addressing climate change through sustainable technology.

Musk's endeavors extend beyond space and automotive technology; his role in Neuralink aims to bridge the gap between humans and machines through brain-computer interfaces. Additionally, The Boring Company addresses urban transportation challenges with innovative tunneling solutions. Each of these ventures not only marks a significant milestone in Musk's career but also highlights his overarching vision for the future of humanity, particularly his ambition for Mars colonization. Through these innovations, Musk continues to inspire a new generation of entrepreneurs and technologists, reshaping public perception of what is achievable in our quest for a sustainable and interplanetary future.

Chapter 5: Tesla Motors: Driving Change
The Birth of Tesla

The inception of Tesla, Inc. can be traced back to 2003, a pivotal year for the automotive industry that marked the beginning of a new era in electric vehicles. Founded by Martin Eberhard and Marc Tarpenning, the company aimed to prove that electric cars could be both high-performance and environmentally friendly. Their vision resonated with a growing concern for climate change and the need for sustainable energy alternatives. Despite the promising foundation, the fledgling company faced numerous challenges, including skepticism from traditional automakers and the significant financial hurdles associated with developing electric vehicle technology.

Elon Musk entered the picture in 2004, after leading an initial round of investment in Tesla. As the largest investor, he quickly became an influential figure within the company, taking on the role of chairman of the board. Musk's vision for Tesla extended beyond the creation of a single electric vehicle; he sought to revolutionize not only the automotive industry but also to catalyze a broader shift towards sustainable energy. His ambition was to establish Tesla as a leader in electric vehicles, paving the way for a future where renewable energy sources would dominate the market.

Under Musk's leadership, Tesla launched its first production vehicle, the Tesla Roadster, in 2008. This sports car was a significant milestone, showcasing the potential of electric vehicles to offer both performance and efficiency. The Roadster's impressive range and acceleration dispelled the stereotype that electric cars were slow and impractical. By leveraging cutting-edge lithium-ion battery technology and a lightweight chassis, Tesla demonstrated that electric vehicles could compete with and even outperform their gasoline counterparts.

As the company grew, so did its ambitions. Musk envisioned a full lineup of electric vehicles, which included sedans, SUVs, and eventually, commercial trucks. The introduction of the Model S in 2012 marked a major turning point for the brand. This luxury sedan not only garnered critical acclaim but also established Tesla's reputation as a serious contender in the automotive market. Musk's relentless focus on innovation led to continuous improvements in battery technology, autonomous driving capabilities, and manufacturing efficiency, positioning Tesla at the forefront of the electric vehicle revolution.

The birth of Tesla signified more than just the launch of a company; it represented a transformative movement towards sustainable transportation. Elon Musk's relentless pursuit of innovation and excellence helped overcome initial skepticism and established Tesla as a symbol of what the future could hold for electric mobility. As the company continued to evolve, it not only changed the landscape of the automotive industry but also inspired a global shift towards renewable energy solutions, setting the stage for a more sustainable future for generations to come.

The Roadster and Its Significance

The Tesla Roadster, launched in 2008, marked a pivotal moment not just in automotive history but also in the broader narrative of sustainable energy and innovation. As the first all-electric sports car, it showcased the potential of electric vehicles to deliver high performance while adhering to environmental standards. By breaking the stereotype that electric cars were slow and unattractive, the Roadster played a crucial role in shifting public perception about electric mobility. It effectively positioned Tesla as a serious player in the automotive industry, setting the stage for the company's future successes and innovations.

One of the significant impacts of the Roadster was its ability to attract attention and investment in electric vehicle technology. At a time when the automotive industry was dominated by traditional combustion engines, the Roadster provided a compelling case for the viability of electric vehicles. This success was instrumental in garnering the necessary funding for Tesla to further develop its technology and expand its lineup. The Roadster's performance metrics, including a 0 to 60 mph time of under four seconds, demonstrated that electric cars could compete with and even surpass their gas-powered counterparts in speed and efficiency.

Moreover, the Roadster laid the groundwork for Tesla's subsequent models, including the Model S, Model X, and Model 3. Each of these vehicles benefited from the technological advancements developed during the Roadster's production. The lessons learned in battery technology, software development, and manufacturing processes were critical in refining Tesla's approach to electric vehicle design. As a result, the Roadster not only served as a prototype for future models but also helped establish Tesla's reputation for innovation and quality.

The significance of the Roadster extends beyond the automotive realm; it symbolizes a shift in consumer expectations and corporate responsibilities towards sustainability. As environmental concerns have become increasingly urgent, the Roadster's introduction represented a proactive approach to addressing climate change through technological advancement. Tesla's marketing of the Roadster as a luxury item that also contributed to a greener planet appealed to a new generation of environmentally conscious consumers, thereby influencing broader trends in the automotive market.

In summary, the Tesla Roadster's impact resonates across multiple facets of modern society, from technology to environmentalism. It not only transformed the perception of electric vehicles but also inspired a new wave of innovation in the automotive industry. As part of Elon Musk's vision for a sustainable future, the Roadster's significance lies in its ability to ignite interest and investment in electric mobility, paving the way for a more sustainable and technologically advanced society.

Transitioning to Sustainable Energy Solutions

The transition to sustainable energy solutions represents a crucial step in addressing the pressing challenges of climate change and resource depletion. As humanity stands on the brink of interplanetary exploration, the lessons learned from Earth's energy crisis can guide the development of sustainable practices on Mars. Elon Musk's initiatives, particularly with Tesla and SolarCity, have laid the groundwork for a comprehensive approach to energy sustainability that combines innovation with practicality. This transition not only aims to reduce dependence on fossil fuels but also promotes renewable energy sources, such as solar and wind, which are vital for supporting human life beyond Earth.

Tesla's evolution from the Roadster to a wide range of electric vehicles illustrates the potential of sustainable technology to revolutionize transportation. The Roadster was not only a proof of concept but also a statement that electric vehicles could be both desirable and high-performing. As Tesla expanded its product line to include more affordable models, it democratized access to electric vehicles, significantly impacting consumer behavior and the automotive industry at large. This shift towards electric mobility serves as a model for future transportation solutions on Mars, where reliance on sustainable energy will be essential for establishing a self-sufficient colony.

Solar energy, a key component of Musk's vision for sustainable energy, has the potential to transform the way we harness and store power, both on Earth and Mars. With advancements in solar panel technology and energy storage solutions like the Powerwall, Musk has demonstrated the feasibility of integrating renewable energy into everyday life. This approach not only addresses energy needs but also emphasizes resilience against the disruptions caused by climate change. On Mars, where sunlight is abundant but harsh environmental conditions exist, effective solar energy systems will be critical to sustaining habitats and powering exploration missions.

Musk's ventures also emphasize the importance of developing sustainable infrastructure that can support energy needs in various contexts. The Boring Company's focus on tunneling technology aims to alleviate urban transportation challenges while simultaneously reducing carbon footprints. By integrating electric vehicle systems with infrastructure designed for efficiency, Musk envisions cities that are less reliant on traditional gas-powered transportation. These principles will be equally applicable in Martian settlements, where the design of habitats and transportation networks must prioritize sustainability to ensure the long-term viability of human life on another planet.

In summary, transitioning to sustainable energy solutions is not merely an Earth-centric goal but a fundamental aspect of Elon Musk's vision for humanity's future, both on our home planet and beyond. By leveraging innovative technologies and sustainable practices, Musk's initiatives showcase the potential for a cleaner, more efficient energy landscape. As we look towards Mars colonization, these advancements will be instrumental in creating a sustainable ecosystem that supports human life, paving the way for a new era of exploration and habitation beyond Earth.

Chapter 6: Neuralink: Bridging Mind and Machine

Founding Neuralink

The founding of Neuralink in 2016 marked a pivotal moment in Elon Musk's ongoing quest to enhance human capabilities and address the challenges posed by artificial intelligence. Musk's concern about the potential dangers of AI, combined with his vision for a more integrated human-technology relationship, led him to explore the frontiers of brain-computer interfaces (BCIs). Neuralink aimed to develop advanced technologies that would allow seamless communication between the human brain and computers, ultimately striving to enable individuals to augment their cognitive abilities and treat neurological disorders.

Neuralink's inception was influenced by Musk's belief that humans must evolve alongside AI to remain relevant in a rapidly changing technological landscape. He posited that as AI systems become more sophisticated, they could surpass human intelligence, creating a potential existential threat. By enhancing human cognitive capabilities through direct brain-machine interfacing, Musk envisioned a future where people could coexist with advanced AI, sharing a symbiotic relationship rather than falling victim to its dominance. This philosophy underpinned Neuralink's mission and attracted a diverse team of engineers, neuroscientists, and medical professionals dedicated to pushing the boundaries of neuroscience and technology.

One of the significant challenges Neuralink faced was the complexity of interfacing with the human brain. The team developed a minimally invasive surgical procedure to implant ultra-thin threads into the brain, capable of reading neural signals with unprecedented precision. This technology aimed to bridge the gap between the brain's intricate neural networks and external devices, paving the way for applications ranging from restoring mobility to individuals with paralysis to enhancing memory and cognitive functions. The ambitious nature of Neuralink's goals underscored Musk's characteristic drive for innovation and his willingness to tackle some of humanity's most pressing challenges.

As Neuralink progressed, it garnered attention not only for its groundbreaking technology but also for the ethical implications surrounding brain-computer interfaces. The prospect of enhancing human capabilities raised questions about privacy, consent, and the potential for socioeconomic divides based on access to such technologies. Musk and his team engaged in ongoing discussions about these ethical considerations, emphasizing the importance of responsible development and deployment of their innovations. This dialogue highlighted Musk's recognition of the complexities involved in merging humanity with technology, a theme that resonates throughout his various ventures.

In the years following its founding, Neuralink has continued to make strides in both research and public awareness, participating in conferences and demonstrations to showcase its achievements. As the company moves closer to its goal of human trials, the potential impact of its innovations on society remains profound. By addressing neurological conditions and enhancing human capabilities, Neuralink embodies Musk's broader vision for a future where humanity not only survives but thrives in an increasingly complex and technologically advanced world. The journey of Neuralink reflects Musk's enduring belief that technology can be harnessed for the betterment of humanity, paving the way for a new era of human evolution.

Goals and Challenges in Brain-Computer Interfaces

The development of brain-computer interfaces (BCIs) represents a significant frontier in technology, one that Elon Musk has identified as critical to the future of human interaction with machines and, ultimately, the colonization of Mars. The primary goal of BCIs is to establish a direct communication pathway between the brain and external devices, thereby allowing for a seamless integration of human cognition with digital systems. This technology holds the potential to revolutionize not only medical treatments for neurological disorders but also enhance human capabilities, making it a pivotal element of Musk's vision for a multi-planetary existence.

One of the major challenges in developing effective BCIs lies in the complexity of the human brain itself. The brain consists of approximately 86 billion neurons, each connected by synapses that form intricate networks responsible for every thought, action, and feeling. Decoding these neural signals in real-time and translating them into meaningful commands for machines is a monumental task. Researchers must navigate various technical hurdles, including signal noise, the biocompatibility of implanted devices, and the need for a non-invasive approach that minimizes risks to users. These challenges require not only advanced engineering solutions but also interdisciplinary collaboration across neuroscience, computer science, and robotics.

Another significant hurdle is ethical and regulatory concerns surrounding the use of BCIs. As the technology progresses, questions arise regarding data privacy, consent, and the potential for misuse or hacking of neural data. The implications of enhancing human capabilities through BCIs also introduce philosophical dilemmas about what it means to be human and the societal implications of creating a divide between those with access to such technology and those without. Addressing these ethical considerations is crucial to fostering public trust and acceptance of BCIs, particularly as Musk envisions their application in everyday life for future Martian settlers.

Despite these challenges, the potential benefits of BCIs are immense. For individuals with disabilities, BCIs could provide unprecedented opportunities for communication and mobility, significantly improving their quality of life. For those on Earth and in future Martian colonies, enhanced cognitive abilities could lead to increased productivity, better decision-making, and even the ability to upload and share thoughts instantaneously. This could pave the way for collaborative efforts that transcend the limitations of physical communication, crucial for survival in the harsh environments of space and on other planets.

In summary, while the journey toward developing effective brain-computer interfaces is fraught with challenges, the potential rewards align closely with Elon Musk's vision of advancing human civilization beyond Earth. By overcoming technical, ethical, and societal barriers, BCIs could transform not only how we interact with technology but also how we understand and enhance the human experience in the cosmos. As this technology evolves, it will undoubtedly play a pivotal role in shaping the future of humanity, whether on Earth or on Mars.

Potential Applications and Ethical Considerations

The potential applications of Elon Musk's vision for human life on Mars extend far beyond the mere act of colonization. They encompass advancements in technology, sustainability, and societal structures that could redefine human existence. For instance, the development of life-support systems suitable for Mars could lead to innovations in closed-loop ecosystems here on Earth, addressing critical issues such as resource scarcity and environmental degradation. Moreover, the technologies developed for Martian habitation might enhance agricultural practices on Earth, contributing to food security as the global population continues to rise.

In addition to technological advancements, Musk's vision raises significant ethical considerations. The prospect of colonizing Mars prompts questions about the rights of potential inhabitants, the preservation of any existing Martian ecosystems, and the implications of creating a society in a new frontier. As humanity looks to establish a presence on another planet, ethical frameworks will need to be developed to govern interactions with the Martian environment and any life forms that may exist there. This includes discussions about terraforming practices and the long-term impacts of human activities on the Martian landscape.

Furthermore, the socio-political dynamics of a Mars colony present intriguing challenges. Musk's vision advocates for a self-sustaining colony that could serve as a backup for humanity, but this raises questions about governance, resource allocation, and social organization. How will laws be established in a new society? Who will have authority, and how will decisions be made? These considerations necessitate a deep exploration of political philosophy and the application of historical lessons learned from Earth's own colonization efforts.

The interplay between technology and ethics is crucial in the context of Musk's endeavors. For instance, the rapid development of artificial intelligence and automation aimed at supporting life on Mars could lead to ethical dilemmas regarding the treatment of machines and the potential displacement of human labor. As neural interfaces and other advanced technologies become integral to life on Mars, society must grapple with the implications of these innovations on human identity and autonomy. Balancing progress with ethical responsibility will be essential to ensuring that the goals of space exploration do not come at the cost of our core human values.

Ultimately, the vision of human life on Mars is not solely a technical challenge; it is a profound opportunity to rethink what it means to live together as a society. The potential applications of Musk's vision, coupled with the ethical considerations it entails, can guide humanity toward a future that is not only technologically advanced but also socially equitable and environmentally sustainable. As we stand on the brink of interplanetary exploration, the lessons learned from these discussions will shape the trajectory of human civilization for generations to come.

Chapter 7: The Boring Company: Rethinking Urban Transport
Conceptualization and Goals

Elon Musk's vision for human life beyond Earth emerges from a profound conceptualization of humanity's future. Central to this vision is the belief that expanding human presence to other planets, particularly Mars, is essential for our survival and evolution. Musk argues that establishing a sustainable human settlement on Mars provides a safeguard against existential threats that could arise on Earth, such as climate change, nuclear warfare, or asteroid impacts. This perspective not only reflects Musk's innovative thinking but also positions interplanetary colonization as a critical goal for the survival of the species.

The goals associated with Musk's vision extend beyond mere survival; they encompass the creation of a self-sustaining city on Mars. Musk envisions a thriving community that would utilize local resources, such as water and minerals, to support its inhabitants. By leveraging technologies developed through SpaceX and other ventures, Musk aims to establish a habitat where humans can live, work, and thrive, thereby paving the way for the eventual terraforming of the planet. This ambition highlights the need for advanced engineering, sustainable practices, and a robust infrastructure capable of supporting life in a harsh extraterrestrial environment.

In pursuit of these goals, Musk has outlined a series of ambitious milestones for SpaceX, including the development of the Starship spacecraft, which is designed for interplanetary travel. The successful launch and landing of prototypes have demonstrated the feasibility of reusable rocket technology, significantly reducing the cost of space travel. Musk's commitment to iterative design and rapid prototyping exemplifies a modern approach to innovation, one that emphasizes learning from failures and continuously refining techniques to meet the ultimate objective of Mars colonization.

Musk's vision is also deeply intertwined with the broader implications for humanity's future. By advocating for the exploration and colonization of Mars, he challenges societal norms and prompts discussions about our role in the universe. This conceptualization of our place in the cosmos underscores the potential for human ingenuity to overcome seemingly insurmountable challenges. Musk's goals encourage a collaborative effort across disciplines, uniting scientists, engineers, and dreamers in the shared pursuit of a multi-planetary existence.

Ultimately, the conceptualization of Mars as a viable destination for human life reflects a synthesis of Musk's ambitions, technological advancements, and philosophical considerations about humanity's future. As we look forward to the possibilities that lie ahead, it is essential to recognize that Musk's vision is not just about reaching another planet; it is about redefining what it means to be human in an ever-expanding universe. The goals set forth by Musk and his companies challenge us to think beyond our current limitations and inspire a new generation to explore, innovate, and dream of a future where Mars awaits.

Major Projects and Innovations

Elon Musk's journey into the realms of innovation and groundbreaking projects is marked by an unyielding ambition to reshape industries and pioneer futuristic technologies. Central to this narrative is SpaceX, founded in 2002, which has achieved remarkable milestones in space exploration. From the successful launch of the Falcon 1 rocket in 2008 to the historic Crew Dragon mission that transported astronauts to the International Space Station in 2020, SpaceX has revolutionized space travel. These achievements not only exemplify Musk's vision of making space more accessible but also highlight the company's focus on reusability, significantly reducing the cost of space missions. The development of the Starship vehicle, designed for interplanetary travel, represents the next frontier in Musk's aspirations for Mars colonization.

In parallel, Tesla has transformed the automotive industry with its innovative approach to electric vehicles and sustainable energy solutions. The introduction of the Tesla Roadster in 2008 marked a pivotal moment, showcasing that electric cars could deliver high performance without compromising on sustainability. Subsequent models, including the Model S, Model 3, and Model X, have further solidified Tesla's reputation as a leader in the electric vehicle market. Beyond vehicles, Tesla's advancements in battery technology and energy storage solutions, such as the Powerwall and Powerpack, have positioned the company at the forefront of the renewable energy movement, aiming to accelerate the world's transition to sustainable energy.

Musk's ventures extend beyond aerospace and automotive industries. Neuralink, founded in 2016, aims to develop brain-computer interfaces that could enhance human capabilities and address neurological disorders. This ambitious project seeks to create a direct communication pathway between the brain and computers, potentially allowing for transformative applications such as memory enhancement, treatment of brain injuries, and even interfacing with artificial intelligence. The implications of Neuralink's innovations could redefine human interaction with technology, blurring the lines between biological and digital realms.

The Boring Company, another of Musk's brainchildren, addresses urban transportation challenges by focusing on tunnel construction and infrastructure. Founded in 2016, the company's goal is to alleviate traffic congestion through innovative tunneling techniques, creating a network of underground transit systems. Projects like the Las Vegas Convention Center Loop showcase the potential of this approach, offering a glimpse into a future where transportation is efficient and less reliant on surface-level congestion. By reimagining how we navigate urban environments, Musk's Boring Company aims to enhance the quality of life in densely populated areas.

Cumulatively, these major projects and innovations reflect Elon Musk's overarching vision for humanity's future. His commitment to interplanetary colonization, sustainable living, and technological integration signifies a profound shift in how we perceive our potential as a species. As Musk continues to push the boundaries of possibility, the impact of his work will likely reverberate through history, shaping the trajectory of modern entrepreneurship and technology. The legacy of these innovations will be critical in understanding the evolution of human life beyond Earth and the role of visionary leaders in that journey.

The Future of Urban Transportation

The future of urban transportation is poised for a radical transformation, driven by innovations that are already emerging from the mind of Elon Musk and his ventures. As cities around the world grapple with congestion, pollution, and the inefficiencies of traditional transport systems, Musk's vision for urban mobility offers compelling solutions. The Boring Company, for example, is at the forefront of this movement with its focus on tunneling technology that aims to alleviate surface traffic. By creating underground transit systems, Musk envisions a future where urban centers can be navigated more efficiently, reducing commute times and enhancing the quality of life for city dwellers.

Electric vehicles (EVs) play a crucial role in this new urban landscape. Tesla has set the standard for EV technology, making it more accessible and desirable for consumers. As urban areas adopt sustainable transportation methods, the proliferation of electric vehicles will contribute to reduced emissions and improved air quality. The integration of smart grid technology with EVs also promises to revolutionize urban transportation, allowing for intelligent energy distribution that supports charging infrastructure and renewable energy sources. This synergy between technology and sustainable practices aligns with Musk's broader vision for a greener planet, both on Earth and beyond.

Moreover, the concept of autonomous vehicles represents a significant leap forward in urban transportation. Tesla's advancements in self-driving technology are paving the way for a future where human error is minimized and road safety is enhanced. With the potential to reduce traffic accidents and streamline traffic flows, autonomous vehicles could fundamentally change how we interact with our urban environment. Musk's vision includes a shift in societal norms regarding vehicle ownership, as ride-sharing services powered by autonomous technology could emerge as a dominant form of transportation, leading to decreased vehicle congestion and better utilization of urban spaces.

In addition to these technological advancements, the design and planning of cities will need to evolve to accommodate new modes of transport. Urban planners will have to rethink infrastructure to support not only electric and autonomous vehicles but also public transit systems that are efficient and user-friendly. This may involve integrating various transportation methods, such as electric scooters, bikes, and mass transit, into a cohesive system that encourages multimodal travel. Musk's influence on this paradigm shift is evident, as his companies strive to create interconnected ecosystems that prioritize sustainable urban mobility.

Ultimately, the future of urban transportation is intricately linked to Musk's broader ambitions for human civilization, both on Earth and in space. By addressing the immediate challenges of urban mobility, Musk sets the stage for humanity's next chapter, wherein efficient transportation will play a critical role in facilitating global connectivity. The innovations spearheaded by Musk not only promise to reshape how we move within cities but also reflect a deeper understanding of our responsibilities toward the environment and the sustainable future of our planet. As we look ahead, the interplay between technology, urban planning, and societal needs will define the next era of transportation, making it a pivotal aspect of Musk's vision for life beyond Earth.

Chapter 8: Musk's Vision for Mars
The Concept of Mars Colonization

The concept of Mars colonization has evolved from a distant dream into a tangible goal, largely fueled by the vision of innovators like Elon Musk. This ambitious endeavor aims to establish a human presence on Mars, addressing both the challenges of life on Earth and the potential for interplanetary habitation. Musk's vision posits that colonizing Mars is not just a necessity for human survival but also a pathway to expanding our civilization beyond the confines of our home planet. By understanding the historical context and technological advancements that have paved the way for this vision, we can appreciate the significance of Mars colonization in the broader narrative of human exploration.

Historically, humanity has always sought to explore the unknown, from the Age of Discovery to the space race of the 20th century. The early missions to the Moon ignited public interest in space exploration and laid the groundwork for future endeavors. As technology progressed, interest shifted towards Mars, with numerous robotic missions revealing the planet's potential for supporting life. Elon Musk recognized this opportunity and founded SpaceX with the express purpose of making interplanetary travel feasible, aiming to inspire a new generation of explorers and scientists to look beyond Earth's boundaries.

The technological innovations spearheaded by SpaceX serve as the backbone for Musk's Mars colonization plans. The development of reusable rocket technology has dramatically reduced the cost of space travel, making it more accessible. The Falcon Heavy and the Starship rockets are pivotal in this framework, designed to carry large payloads and humans to Mars. SpaceX's advancements in life support systems, habitat construction, and sustainable fuel sources are crucial for creating a self-sustaining colony on Mars. Musk envisions a thriving Martian community that can support human life and contribute to the larger goal of making humanity a multiplanetary species.

Musk's vision for Mars colonization extends beyond mere survival; it encompasses the idea of creating a new society that embodies the best of humanity. He advocates for a Martian civilization that prioritizes sustainability, innovation, and cooperation. By establishing a base on Mars, Musk aims to create a platform for scientific research and technological development that could benefit both Mars and Earth. This vision encourages collaboration among nations and private entities, fostering a spirit of unity in the pursuit of a common goal—exploration and survival.

As humanity stands on the brink of a new era in space exploration, the concept of Mars colonization prompts us to reconsider our relationship with our planet and the universe. Elon Musk's relentless pursuit of this dream not only challenges our technological capabilities but also invites us to reflect on our role as stewards of Earth and potential inhabitants of other worlds. The journey toward Mars is not merely about reaching another planet; it is about the evolution of human consciousness and the desire to explore, innovate, and ultimately transcend our limitations. By embracing this vision, we can inspire future generations to continue pushing the boundaries of what is possible in our quest for knowledge and existence beyond Earth.

Technological Requirements for Interplanetary Travel

Interplanetary travel presents a unique set of technological requirements that extend beyond our current capabilities. As we look to the future of human life on Mars, it is essential to understand the advancements needed to make this vision a reality. Key areas of focus include propulsion systems, life support mechanisms, habitat construction, and sustainable energy sources. Each of these components plays a critical role in ensuring the safety and well-being of astronauts on long-duration missions away from Earth.

Propulsion systems are at the forefront of interplanetary travel technology. Current rocket systems, while successful at reaching low Earth orbit, require significant enhancements to enable efficient travel to Mars. SpaceX has been developing the Starship, designed with advanced engines capable of deep space travel. Achieving faster travel times will not only reduce the duration of missions but also minimize the exposure of astronauts to cosmic radiation and other hazards of space travel. Innovations such as in-space refueling and reusable spacecraft are crucial elements in this technological evolution.

Life support systems are equally critical for sustaining human life during interplanetary journeys. These systems must manage air, water, and food supplies over extended periods. Closed-loop life support systems, which recycle waste materials into usable resources, will be essential. Research into growing food in space and creating breathable air from carbon dioxide will enable astronauts to live comfortably on Mars.

The integration of these technologies will ensure that human crews can survive and thrive in the harsh environment of another planet.

The construction of habitats on Mars also presents significant technological challenges. Structures must be designed to withstand extreme temperatures, radiation, and dust storms while providing a livable environment. 3D printing technology has emerged as a promising solution, allowing for the on-site construction of habitats using Martian resources. This approach not only reduces the need to transport building materials from Earth but also paves the way for sustainable living conditions for future colonists.

Sustainable energy sources will be vital for interplanetary settlements, as reliance on Earth-based resources is impractical. Solar energy is a primary candidate, given Mars' proximity to the sun and advancements in solar technology. Developing efficient energy storage systems will ensure that habitats and equipment have a constant power supply, regardless of the time of day or seasonal changes on Mars. By addressing these technological requirements, Elon Musk's vision for Mars colonization can transition from a distant dream to an achievable goal, opening the door to a new era of human exploration and habitation beyond Earth.

The Long-term Vision

The long-term vision that Elon Musk has laid out for humanity encompasses not just the colonization of Mars, but a profound transformation in how we understand our place in the universe. Musk has consistently articulated a future where human beings are a multi-planetary species, fundamentally altering the trajectory of human existence. This vision is rooted in a belief that the survival of humanity may depend on our ability to establish a self-sustaining colony on Mars, creating a backup for civilization in the event of catastrophic events on Earth. By prioritizing interplanetary exploration, Musk aims to inspire a collective pursuit of knowledge and adventure, pushing the boundaries of human capability.

Achieving this ambitious goal requires a comprehensive approach, blending technological innovation with strategic collaboration. SpaceX, Musk's aerospace company, has pioneered advancements in rocket technology, notably with the Falcon 9 and Starship, designed to make space travel more affordable and efficient. These innovations are crucial to reducing the costs associated with sending humans and cargo to Mars. Musk envisions a fleet of Starships regularly shuttling between Earth and Mars, laying the groundwork for a vibrant, sustainable human presence on the red planet. The development of life support systems, habitats, and sustainable agricultural practices will also be essential components of this vision.

Furthermore, Musk's vision for Mars is not solely about survival; it encompasses the creation of a new society that reflects our highest aspirations. He envisions a Martian colony that fosters cooperation, creativity, and innovation, serving as a model for a more harmonious existence. The societal structures established on Mars could potentially address some of the challenges faced on Earth, such as resource scarcity and environmental degradation. Through this lens, the colonization of Mars becomes a profound opportunity to rethink and reshape human civilization, encouraging a new era of exploration and discovery.

The long-term vision Musk presents is supported by his multifaceted approach to entrepreneurship and technology. His work with Tesla has not only revolutionized the automotive industry but has also laid the groundwork for sustainable energy solutions that could benefit both Earth and Mars. The development of technologies like solar energy and battery storage reflects Musk's commitment to creating a sustainable future, which is integral to the survival of any Martian colony. By leveraging the synergies between electric vehicles, energy storage, and space travel, Musk envisions a framework that supports life on multiple planets.

Ultimately, Musk's long-term vision invites us to consider not just the logistics of living on Mars, but the philosophical implications of becoming a multi-planetary species. It challenges us to think about our responsibilities to both Earth and Mars, fostering a dialogue about ethics, governance, and the future of humanity. As we stand on the brink of this new frontier, Musk's vision serves as a catalyst for innovation and optimism, encouraging individuals and societies to embrace the unknown and strive for greatness in the cosmos.

Chapter 9: The Impact of Musk on Entrepreneurship

Redefining Startups and Innovation

In the context of Elon Musk's ventures, the concept of startups and innovation has undergone significant transformation. Traditionally, startups were viewed primarily as small businesses with the potential for rapid growth, often focused on achieving profitability within a short time frame. However, Musk has redefined this model by emphasizing ambitious, long-term goals that prioritize groundbreaking innovation over immediate financial returns. His companies embody a vision that transcends conventional metrics of success, focusing instead on addressing global challenges and exploring new frontiers, particularly in space and sustainable energy.

Musk's early experiences, particularly with Zip2 and later PayPal, laid the groundwork for his understanding of innovation as a driver of change. These ventures taught him the importance of scalability and the potential of technology to disrupt established industries. The success of PayPal, in particular, illustrated how a startup could not only challenge but also transform traditional banking and payment systems. This experience instilled in Musk a belief that startups should aim not just to create products, but to foster systemic change in society, paving the way for his future endeavors in space travel and renewable energy.

SpaceX serves as a prime example of Musk's redefined approach to startups. The company was founded with the audacious goal of reducing space transportation costs and enabling the colonization of Mars. This vision is not solely about making a profit; it is about ensuring the survival of humanity and expanding our species beyond Earth. SpaceX's innovations, such as the reusable rocket, exemplify how Musk has shifted the paradigm of what a startup can achieve. Instead of focusing on incremental improvements, SpaceX's breakthroughs have fundamentally altered the landscape of space exploration, making it more accessible and sustainable.

Similarly, Tesla's journey from the Roadster to a leader in sustainable energy illustrates the expansive view of innovation that Musk advocates. While many startups settle for niche markets, Tesla sought to redefine the entire automotive industry by proving that electric vehicles can be desirable, high-performance, and environmentally friendly. This bold approach demonstrates how Musk has leveraged his influence to push the boundaries of what is possible, inspiring a broader movement toward sustainability in transportation and energy consumption.

Ultimately, Musk's vision for startups extends beyond individual companies; it encompasses a broader philosophy that urges entrepreneurs to pursue visionary goals that can reshape the world. This paradigm shift encourages a culture of risk-taking and resilience, where the potential for failure is viewed not as a deterrent but as an integral part of the innovation process. By redefining what it means to be a startup in the modern era, Musk has inspired a new generation of entrepreneurs to think big and aim for solutions that could one day enable humanity to thrive on Mars and beyond.

Influence on Future Generations of Entrepreneurs

Elon Musk's journey as an entrepreneur has left an indelible mark on the landscape of modern business and technology, inspiring countless individuals to pursue their own innovative ventures. His multi-faceted career, which encompasses groundbreaking companies like SpaceX and Tesla, serves as a blueprint for aspiring entrepreneurs. Musk's relentless pursuit of ambitious goals—such as the colonization of Mars and the development of sustainable energy—has shifted the paradigm of what is possible in entrepreneurship. This influence extends beyond mere business success; it encompasses a vision for humanity's future that encourages risk-taking, creativity, and resilience among future generations.

The principles Musk champions—disruption, innovation, and a willingness to tackle seemingly insurmountable challenges—have become hallmarks of contemporary entrepreneurship. His approach to problem-solving emphasizes the importance of thinking outside traditional frameworks and harnessing technology to drive change. This mindset resonates particularly with young entrepreneurs, who are increasingly motivated to create solutions that address global issues such as climate change and resource scarcity. By showcasing how technology can be leveraged to overcome these challenges, Musk has instilled a sense of purpose in the entrepreneurial spirit, encouraging future leaders to pursue ventures that align with their values and aspirations.

Musk's ventures also highlight the significance of interdisciplinary knowledge in entrepreneurship. His work spans various fields, from aerospace engineering to automotive design and renewable energy. This integration of diverse disciplines inspires future entrepreneurs to embrace a holistic approach to innovation, fostering a culture of collaboration and cross-pollination of ideas. As educational institutions increasingly focus on interdisciplinary studies, Musk's influence reinforces the idea that the next generation of innovators must be adaptable and well-versed in multiple domains to succeed in an ever-evolving landscape.

Moreover, Musk's public persona and media representation play a critical role in shaping perceptions of entrepreneurship. His bold statements and ambitious goals often capture headlines, sparking discussions about the nature of success and the responsibilities of entrepreneurs. By navigating both triumphs and controversies, Musk exemplifies the complexities of modern entrepreneurship, illustrating that the journey is rarely linear. This narrative encourages future entrepreneurs to embrace their unique paths, understanding that setbacks can be valuable learning experiences that contribute to personal and professional growth.

Ultimately, the influence of Elon Musk on future generations of entrepreneurs is profound and multifaceted. His commitment to innovation and exploration inspires a new wave of thinkers who are ready to challenge the status quo. As young entrepreneurs look to Musk's achievements and philosophies, they are motivated to dream bigger and act boldly, pushing the boundaries of what is conceivable. This legacy not only shapes the future of entrepreneurship but also holds the potential to redefine humanity's relationship with technology, sustainability, and the cosmos itself.

Lessons from Musk's Career

Elon Musk's career provides a rich tapestry of lessons that can inspire and instruct future entrepreneurs and innovators. One of the most significant lessons is the importance of resilience in the face of failure. Musk faced numerous challenges early in his career, particularly with Zip2 and later with X.com, which eventually became PayPal. The difficulties he encountered, including financial crises and management disputes, taught him that perseverance is crucial. Instead of allowing setbacks to define him, Musk used them as opportunities to learn and adapt, demonstrating that resilience is a vital trait for anyone pursuing ambitious goals.

Another essential takeaway from Musk's journey is the value of visionary thinking combined with practical execution. Musk has always aimed for the stars, literally and figuratively, with grand visions such as colonizing Mars and revolutionizing transportation. However, he pairs these aspirations with concrete plans and actions. For instance, SpaceX's development of reusable rockets not only reflects innovative thinking but also addresses the practical realities of costs and sustainability in space exploration. This balance of high-level vision and attention to detail is a lesson that can be applied across various fields.

Musk's approach to risk-taking is also noteworthy. He has consistently put his own capital on the line, risking his fortune for the companies he believed in. This willingness to take calculated risks is a critical lesson for entrepreneurs. Musk's investments in Tesla and SpaceX, especially during times of financial uncertainty, illustrate the potential rewards of bold decisions. However, this kind of risk-taking is not without its own set of challenges, and aspiring innovators must carefully weigh the potential benefits against the risks involved.

Collaboration and building a strong team are integral components of Musk's success. He has surrounded himself with talented individuals who share his vision and drive. At SpaceX and Tesla, the emphasis on teamwork and a shared commitment to goals has helped propel these companies forward. This focus on collaboration highlights the importance of nurturing relationships and creating an environment where creativity and innovation can flourish. For anyone looking to make an impact, recognizing the strength of a united team can be a game-changer.

Finally, Musk's journey underscores the significance of public perception and media representation in shaping a career. Musk has experienced both adulation and criticism from the public and media, which has influenced his companies and projects. His ability to navigate this complex landscape while maintaining a clear vision is a critical lesson. Understanding how public perception can affect business outcomes is vital for anyone looking to make their mark, emphasizing the need for effective communication and engagement with stakeholders. Musk's career is a testament to the interplay between vision, resilience, risk, collaboration, and public perception, offering valuable insights for future generations.

Chapter 10: Public Perception of Elon Musk

Media Representation Over Time

Media representation of Elon Musk has evolved significantly over the years, reflecting changing public perceptions and the development of his various ventures. Initially, Musk was introduced to the public as a tech entrepreneur with a knack for innovation, primarily through his work with Zip2 and PayPal. During this early phase, media narratives often focused on his business acumen and the potential of his companies to revolutionize the tech landscape. Coverage tended to highlight his achievements, portraying him as a visionary without delving deeply into his personal life or the controversies that would later arise.

As Musk transitioned into the aerospace industry with SpaceX and the automotive world with Tesla, media narratives began to shift. Coverage increasingly emphasized not just his business successes, but also his ambitious goals for space exploration and sustainable energy. This period marked a significant increase in media interest, with outlets frequently highlighting the groundbreaking nature of his projects. The portrayal of Musk became more complex, as journalists started to explore the implications of his work on society and the environment, while also raising questions about the feasibility of his grand visions.

The rise of social media further transformed Musk's media representation. His direct engagement with the public on platforms like Twitter allowed him to shape his own narrative, often bypassing traditional media gatekeepers. This accessibility created a dual-edged sword; while it endeared him to many fans who appreciated his candidness and humor, it also exposed him to criticism and scrutiny. Incidents such as controversial tweets and public statements led to mixed media portrayals, oscillating between admiration for his genius and concern over his impulsiveness.

In recent years, as Musk's projects have matured and his ambitions have grown bolder, media representation has begun to reflect a more nuanced view of the entrepreneur. Coverage now often includes a critical lens, examining the ethical implications of his ventures, such as the impact of Tesla's manufacturing practices or the challenges faced by SpaceX in its pursuit of Mars colonization. While Musk is still celebrated for his innovative spirit, there is a growing recognition of the complexities surrounding his leadership style and the societal consequences of his technological advancements.

Looking ahead, the future of Musk's media representation will likely continue to evolve in tandem with his endeavors. As humanity stands on the brink of potential interplanetary colonization, Musk's role as a pioneer in this new frontier will be scrutinized through various lenses, including those of ethics, sustainability, and corporate responsibility. Ultimately, how the media portrays Musk will reflect broader societal attitudes toward technology and its capacity to shape human life beyond Earth. The interplay between Musk's ambitions and public perception will shape not only his legacy but also the narratives surrounding the future of space exploration and innovation.

Public Reactions to Musk's Ventures

Public reactions to Elon Musk's ventures have been as varied and dynamic as the projects themselves. From the early days of Zip2 to the ambitious plans for Mars colonization, the public has oscillated between admiration and skepticism. Initial excitement surrounding Musk's foray into the tech world was palpable, particularly with the launch of PayPal, which revolutionized online payments. As Musk transitioned from software to space exploration with SpaceX, public interest surged, fueled by the audacity of his goals and the spectacle of rocket launches. Each milestone achieved by SpaceX, such as the successful Falcon 1 launch and the first privately-funded spacecraft to reach orbit, garnered significant media coverage, further shaping public perception of Musk as a visionary.

As Tesla emerged as a front-runner in electric vehicles, public reactions became increasingly polarized. Advocates hailed Musk as a pioneer in sustainable energy, praising his commitment to reducing carbon footprints and promoting renewable technologies. Conversely, critics pointed to production challenges, safety concerns, and the financial viability of Tesla's business model. This duality in public opinion reflects broader societal debates about technological innovation, environmental responsibility, and the future of transportation. Social media platforms amplified these discussions, allowing both supporters and detractors to voice their opinions, often in real-time, further contributing to Musk's complex public image.

Neuralink, Musk's venture into brain-computer interfaces, sparked considerable intrigue and apprehension. While some embraced the potential for groundbreaking medical advancements, others expressed ethical concerns regarding privacy, consent, and the implications of merging human cognition with technology. The public reaction highlighted a deep-seated ambivalence towards rapid technological change, especially when it intersects with fundamental aspects of human identity. This discourse demonstrated a growing awareness of the societal consequences of Musk's innovations, illustrating that public engagement with his projects is not merely passive but involves active discourse on ethical and existential issues.

The Boring Company, aimed at alleviating urban traffic woes, received mixed responses as well. While many urban dwellers welcomed innovative solutions to congestion, skeptics questioned the feasibility and safety of underground transportation systems. The public's reaction was indicative of a broader trend towards viewing Musk's ventures as emblematic of a new era of entrepreneurial ambition that challenges traditional infrastructure paradigms. This venture, like others, reflects Musk's penchant for high-risk, high-reward projects, eliciting both enthusiasm for progress and concern about the implications of such disruption.

Overall, Musk's ventures have sparked a continuous dialogue about innovation, ethics, and the future of humanity. The interplay between public perception and media representation has played a crucial role in shaping the narrative around Musk, who, despite facing criticism and skepticism, has consistently pushed the boundaries of what is possible. As he continues to pursue his vision for human life beyond Earth, public reactions will undoubtedly evolve, reflecting the complexities of technological advancement and the human experience in the face of unprecedented change.

The Duality of Celebrity and Controversy

The relationship between celebrity and controversy is a defining aspect of Elon Musk's public persona, shaping both his personal brand and the perception of his ventures. As a figure who has consistently pushed boundaries across various industries, from electric vehicles to space travel, Musk often finds himself at the intersection of innovation and public scrutiny. His bold statements and ambitious projects draw significant media attention, not just for their potential impact on technology and society but also for the controversies that often accompany them. This duality has made him a polarizing figure, attracting both fervent supporters and staunch critics.

Musk's rise to fame began with his involvement in PayPal, where his innovative approach to online banking helped revolutionize financial transactions. This success laid the groundwork for his subsequent ventures, each of which further solidified his status as a celebrity entrepreneur. However, with fame came scrutiny. His unfiltered communication style, particularly on social media, has sparked numerous controversies that often overshadow his achievements. Statements that might be seen as visionary by some can be interpreted as reckless or irresponsible by others, illustrating how his celebrity status amplifies the repercussions of his words and actions.

SpaceX, one of Musk's most ambitious projects, exemplifies this duality well. The company has achieved remarkable milestones in space exploration, such as the successful launch and landing of reusable rockets, which have transformed the economics of space travel. Yet, Musk's approach to publicizing these achievements has sometimes led to misunderstandings and critiques. His ambitious timelines and bold predictions often generate skepticism, and when delays occur, they fuel further controversy. The media's portrayal of these events can swing dramatically, highlighting the tension between Musk's visionary goals and the realities of technological development.

Tesla's evolution from the Roadster to a leader in sustainable energy is another case study in the interplay of celebrity and controversy. The company's mission to accelerate the world's transition to sustainable energy resonates with many, yet Musk's management style and public behavior have sparked debates about corporate governance and ethical leadership. Incidents such as his comments about taking Tesla private have led to regulatory scrutiny, illustrating how Musk's celebrity can complicate the narrative around his companies. The resulting controversies can distract from the innovative work being done within Tesla, often shifting the focus from technological advancements to personal missteps.

Ultimately, the duality of celebrity and controversy surrounding Elon Musk reflects broader societal attitudes toward innovation and risk-taking. As a trailblazer in multiple industries, Musk embodies the potential for transformative change, yet his public persona invites ongoing debate about accountability and responsibility. The complexities of this relationship influence not only his legacy but also the future of the industries he seeks to disrupt. By examining both his achievements and the controversies that accompany them, we gain a deeper understanding of the challenges and opportunities that characterize the journey toward a future where human life extends beyond Earth.

Don't miss out!

Visit the website below and you can sign up to receive emails whenever Stephen G. publishes a new book. There's no charge and no obligation.

https://books2read.com/r/B-A-VPPMC-OMRDF

BOOKS 2 READ

Connecting independent readers to independent writers.